SCIENCE

CURIOUS
Questions and Answers

SCIENCE

CURIOUS
Questions and Answers

Words by Camilla de la Bédoyère and Anne Rooney

Illustrations by Pauline Reeves, Ana Gomez
and Tim Budgen (including cover)

MILES KELLY

First published in 2020 by Miles Kelly Publishing Ltd
Harding's Barn, Bardfield End Green, Thaxted, Essex, CM6 3PX, UK

Copyright © Miles Kelly Publishing Ltd 2020

2 4 6 8 10 9 7 5 3 1

Publishing Director Belinda Gallagher

Creative Director Jo Cowan

Editorial Director Rosie Neave

Senior Editors Amy Johnson, Becky Miles

Designers Rob Hale, Joe Jones, Simon Lee

Image Manager Liberty Newton

Production Elizabeth Collins, Jennifer Brunwin-Jones

Reprographics Stephan Davis

Assets Lorraine King

ISBN 978-1-78989-151-5

Printed in China

British Library Cataloguing-in-Publication Data
A catalogue record for this book is available from the British Library

Made with paper from a sustainable forest

www.mileskelly.net

CONTENTS

SCIENCE

How do we find things out?

We know about the world around us because scientists look carefully and carry out experiments. You could be a scientist! All you have to do is...

① Spot a problem

Keep your eyes and ears open. Look out for questions to ask and problems to solve.

② Have an idea

Think of something that could explain or solve the problem. This is your theory.

③ Design an experiment

Work out how to test your idea – an experiment. Change just one thing at a time to make a fair test.

④ Check what happens

Were you right? If not, you might need a new theory and a new experiment.

① Long ago, sailors were often ill with a disease called scurvy.

These long journeys are killing me! Can't somebody do something?

② Scientist James Lind (1716–1794) decided to investigate.

I think it might be what you're eating – or what you're not eating.

③ Cider

Oranges and lemons

Sea water

It's worth a try...

Vinegar

Lind chose six pairs of sick sailors. All had the same food, except he gave each pair one extra thing.

④ Months later, the sailors who had oranges and lemons were better. The rest were even more sick.

I want what he had!

Why do we need scientists?

The work of scientists can make life better. A discovery can lead to more questions and experiments. Science keeps on going.

Modern scientists found out that it is the Vitamin C in fruit that stops scurvy.

Do plants eat?

Plants don't eat like animals do – they use sunlight to make their own food in their leaves.

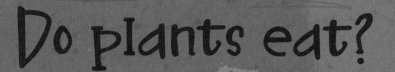

Sunflower

All living things need energy. We get ours from sunlight. We use this energy to turn water and gas into food.

I can't grow in the shade, as I'm not getting the sunlight I need.

Plants don't breathe like you, but gases go in and out through their leaves.

Sunlight acts on chemicals in the plant's leaves to make food.

What use are roots?

Roots keep plants fixed in the soil so they don't fall over or blow away! Through their roots, plants take in water and small amounts of chemicals from the soil. Roots also store food for the plant.

Secondary roots

Main root

How are new plants made?

Most plants reproduce – make baby plants – by producing seeds.

The seeds fall to the ground, blow away in the wind, or are spread by animals to new places to grow.

Dandelion seeds

Dandelion

Some plants make fruit with seeds in. Animals eat the fruit. The seeds come out in their poo, ready to grow somewhere else.

Parent strawberry plant

Runner

New strawberry plant

Certain types of plants grow baby plants on special stalks called runners. The new plants then grow their own roots and the runner drops off.

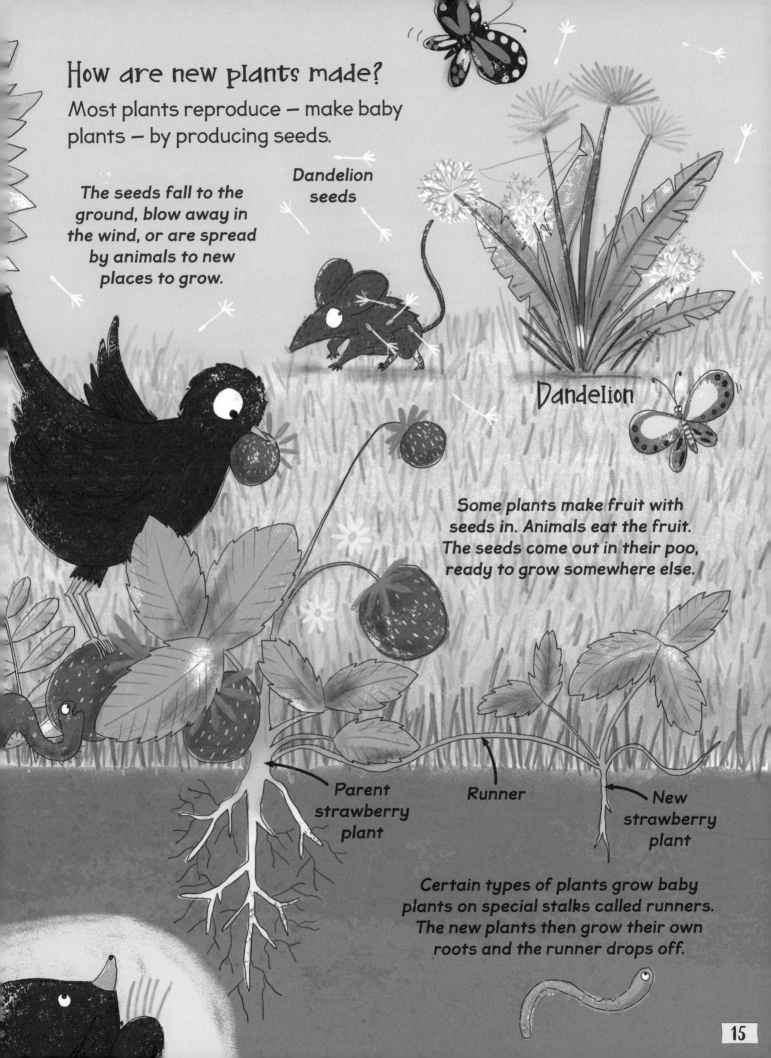

How many?

320

The number of days it would take to drive to the Moon non-stop at 50 kilometres per hour.

60–70

The percentage of your body that is water.

300,000,000

The speed in metres per second that light travels.

3%

How much taller an astronaut is in space where gravity is not pulling their body downwards.

50%

The proportion of cells in your body that are not you, but germs and other micro organisms.

A skydiver can reach a speed of **195** kilometres per hour.

1,000,000,000,000,000,000,000,000

Roughly how many stars there are in the known Universe.

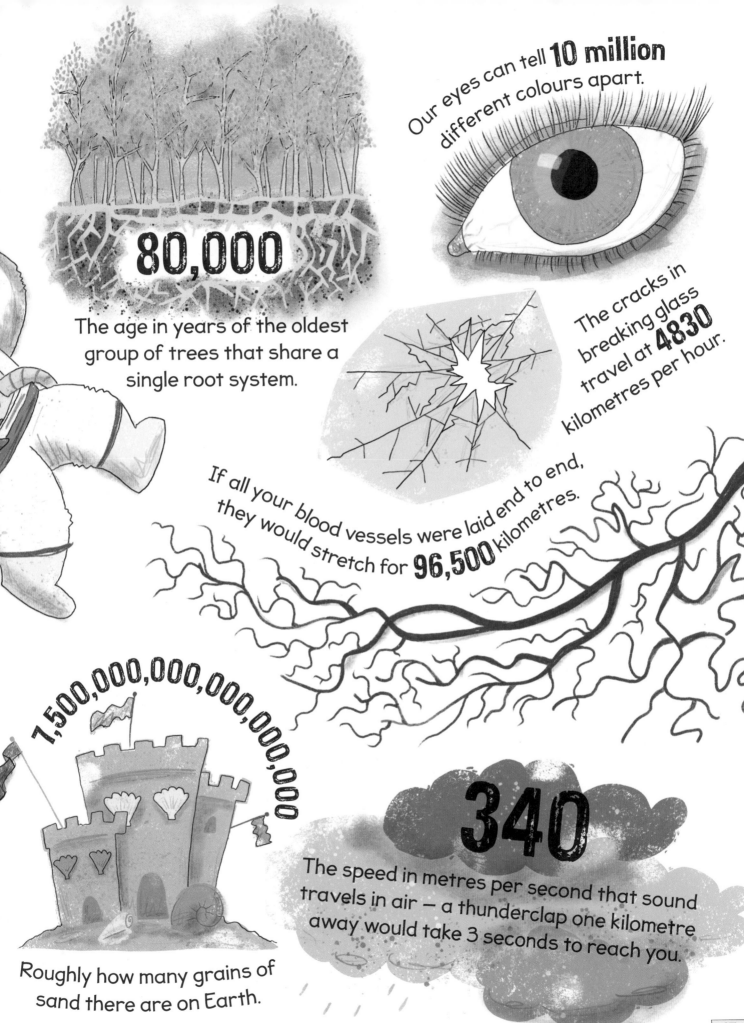

Our eyes can tell **10 million** different colours apart.

80,000

The age in years of the oldest group of trees that share a single root system.

The cracks in breaking glass travel at **4830** kilometres per hour.

If all your blood vessels were laid end to end, they would stretch for **96,500** kilometres.

1,500,000,000,000,000,000,000

Roughly how many grains of sand there are on Earth.

340

The speed in metres per second that sound travels in air — a thunderclap one kilometre away would take 3 seconds to reach you.

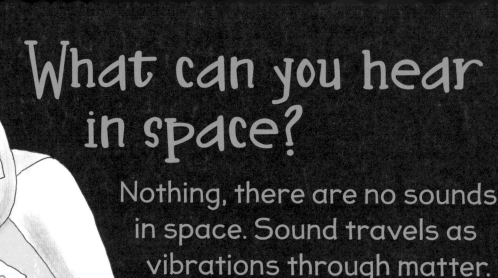

What can you hear in space?

Nothing, there are no sounds in space. Sound travels as vibrations through matter. As space is empty, there is nothing for sound to travel through.

I can hear noises inside my suit and in my headset but not from outside. Anything could sneak up on me!

Dolphins can hear much higher sounds than humans!

Why do things sound different underwater?

The vibrations are going through water, not air, making things sound a bit different. We can hear higher sounds in water than in air.

Dolphins use sound to hunt for food and find their way underwater. They make noises such as clicks and buzzes.

Do we all hear the same sounds?

No – children can hear higher and lower sounds than grown-ups. You can probably hear bats squeaking and high-pitched dog whistles, when older people hear nothing.

Can you hear the people?

Can you hear the bats?

Sri Lanka

Indian Ocean

New Guinea

East Africa

Krakatau

Australia

The eruption was so loud, it could be heard in all these places!

What's the loudest sound ever?

A volcano called Krakatau erupted in Indonesia in 1883, making the loudest sound humans have ever heard. It could be heard 5000 kilometres away.

How does electricity get to my house?

Electricity is a type of energy. It is generated in power stations then carried along a network of cables, all the way to the wires and power points throughout your house.

Lots of things we use every day, such as lights and computers, are powered by electricity. It makes the fridge cold, and the heater hot!

Can you spot some other objects that need electricity to work?

How is electricity made?

We get electricity by changing other forms of energy such as sunlight, wind, moving water, or by burning coal, oil or gas.

Coal, oil and gas are known as fossil fuels, because they come from the remains of animals and plants that lived long ago. A lot of our energy comes from burning fossil fuels.

Wires inside the walls carry electricity to all the places it's needed. We plug electrical objects into sockets in the wall.

Fossil fuels will run out in the future, and burning them causes pollution. So people are trying to use more energy from sources that can't be used up.

Solar power

Energy from sunlight is captured in solar panels and changed into electricity.

Water power

The energy of water held by a dam is changed into electrical energy.

Wind power

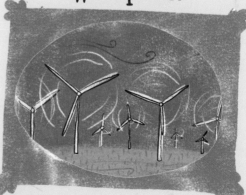

Wind turbines change the wind's movement energy into electricity.

Why do I feel ill?

Many illnesses are caused by germs – tiny things too small to see. There are germs everywhere. Your body tries to keep them out, and is good at fighting them when they get in.

How does my body fight germs?

It makes special cells (tiny parts of your body) that attack germs and anything else that shouldn't be inside you.

③ They destroy the germs by swallowing them whole!

② Special body cells come to the rescue by attacking the germs.

① Once inside your body, germs set up home and start reproducing – soon there are lots and lots.

What is a fever?

You might feel hot when you're ill. Your body pushes its temperature up to kill off germs that don't like the heat. This doesn't feel good, but it does you good!

Can I get the same type of germ again?

When you catch an illness like chickenpox, your body learns how to fight it. You probably won't get it again: if another chickenpox germ comes along, your body can deal with it quickly — it doesn't stand a chance.

While your body is fighting germs, you might feel ill. You might be sick, feel too hot, cough, sneeze or have aches and pains.

Did you know?

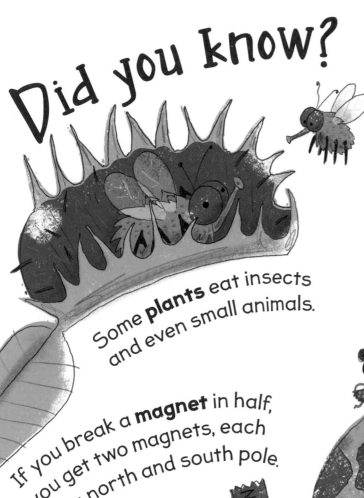

Some **plants** eat insects and even small animals.

There are **meteorites** — tiny bits of rock from space — all around. One hits each square metre of ground about once a year.

If you break a **magnet** in half, you get two magnets, each with a north and south pole.

If we could drill a hole right through the **Earth**, things wouldn't fall straight through; they would get to the middle and stop.

Nine tenths of an **iceberg** is under water. Ice only just floats, so not much sticks out.

If you put a **carnation** in coloured water, it will eventually suck up the water and turn the same colour.

Bamboo grows so fast you can watch it get taller. It can grow 91 centimetres in a single day.

If there was no air, a **feather** and **cricket ball** dropped from the same height would hit the ground together.

The **Apollo spacecraft** were landed on the Moon by a computer less powerful than a smartphone.

The largest land animal ever was **Patagotitan**, a dinosaur that weighed about 70 tonnes and was 37 metres long.

I weighed about the same as 12 African elephants!

Some **volcanic rocks** float on water. This is because they are full of air bubbles.

If you float a **needle** on water it lines up to point north/south.

Earth's continents move slowly all the time, so the **Atlantic Ocean** grows a few centimetres wider each year.

Why do I have a shadow?

Your body blocks light coming from the Sun or a lamp, making a darker patch on the other side.

Why is my reflection the wrong way round?

Light from the left side of your body travels to the mirror and bounces off, making the left side of your reflection.

If you were standing where your reflection is, that would be your right side, so it looks the wrong way round.

What makes a rainbow?

If sunlight (white light) passes through raindrops at the right angle, it is split up into a spectrum of colours inside the raindrops. The colours come out in different directions.

You see one colour from each raindrop — which colour depends on the angle you are looking at the raindrop. All together they make stripes — a rainbow!

Red
Orange
Yellow
Green
Blue
Indigo
Violet

Why can't I see round corners?

Light always travels in straight lines. You can see round corners, but only if you bounce the light around a bit using mirrors. This is how a periscope in a submarine works.

Mirror

Light

Mirror

What eats lions?

A few things nibble lions – like biting insects – and crocodiles sometimes kill lions. But mostly lions eat other animals. The world is full of creatures that eat each other.

What do herbivores eat?

Herbivores are animals that eat plants. They can be big – like us giraffes – or tiny – like bugs and birds.

How do animals make a chain?

The order in which animals eat each other – and plants – is called a food chain. It's easy to see who eats who.

Biting fly

Lion

Antelope

Grass

Most animals don't eat only one thing. Food chains fit together into a food web.

An omnivore is an animal that is able to eat both plants and other animals. Are you a carnivore, herbivore or omnivore?

Whose food is already dead?

Some creatures, such as vultures, eat carrion – animals that have already died. Vultures will eat the dead lion one day – and so will tiny bugs and worms.

What is a carnivore?

Carnivores are animals that eat other animals. Lions eat zebras, antelope and sometimes young giraffes.

Which animals help hippos?

These oxpeckers help me by eating the insects that bite my skin. This helps them because they get a good meal!

Why do things fall?

The force of gravity pulls objects towards the centre of the Earth – downwards! Gravity is everywhere in the Universe, pulling things with less mass towards things with more mass. The Earth has more mass than anything on it.

Gravity →

Things only move if a force acts on them. You can think of forces as 'Pushes' or 'Pulls'. I'm falling because gravity is pulling me down.

← Drag

Why does a parachute slow your fall?

A force called drag acts on the parachute. When the parachute opens, air is trapped under it. The air has to be pushed out of the way for the parachute to fall. The air holds the parachute up while gravity pulls it down.

How does a magnet stick your picture to the fridge?

Some metals are magnetic (they will stick to a magnet). Magnetism is a force that can act even through thin layers that are not magnetic — like paper.

Which force stops you slipping?

Friction is a force between surfaces that stops them sliding over each other. On ice, there is very little friction. There is more between rough surfaces, so your shoes grip to a rough road surface and slip on ice.

How many magnetic objects can you find in your home?

Ice skates have super-smooth blades to cut down friction — that means I go faster!

milk
bread
Jam

Gravity

Would you rather?

Would you rather be a **vulture** that eats dead animals or a **worm** that eats soil?

If you were a superhero, would you rather have enough **friction** to walk up walls or be able to turn **gravity** off and float around?

Would it be better to be able to see **round corners** or in the **dark**?

Would you prefer to study **tigers** in the jungle or explore scary **volcanoes**?

Would you rather invent an amazing new **material** or design a fantastic **vehicle**?

Would you rather be **super-stretchy** like elastic, or **super-springy** and bounce everywhere?

Time for adventure! Would you rather be an **astronaut** going to Mars or a **diver** exploring the deepest oceans?

Would you rather be so **light** you can walk on water...

...or so **dense** you could walk along the seabed?

Gravity

A ship made of solid metal, without any air in it, would sink.

Buoyancy

Which force pushes up?

Buoyancy! Buoyancy is a force that pushes upwards through a fluid (such as water or air) against the weight of an object. When the weight pushing down (gravity) and the buoyancy are equal, the object doesn't move up or down.

Why do ships float?

Whether something sinks or floats depends on its density (how heavy something is for its volume). Most big ships are made of metal. Metal is more dense than water, but a ship floats because it is mostly full of air.

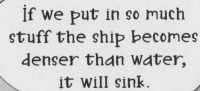

If we put in so much stuff the ship becomes denser than water, it will sink.

Do fish sink or float?

They can do both! Fish are almost the same density as water. Many types have a swim bladder, which is a sac filled with gas in their stomach. The amount of gas controls the fish's buoyancy to keep it at the right level in the water. It can add more gas to go up, or lose gas to go down.

What is matter?

Matter is everything around you! It has three states: a solid, a liquid, or a gas.

Solid
A solid (like paper, wood or plastic) can hold its shape.

Liquid
A liquid can't hold its shape. It spreads out into a pool unless it's held in a container.

The gas in my balloon can't get out.

Gas
A gas doesn't hold its shape. It spreads out as far as possible. To keep a gas in one place, we put it in a closed container.

Why does ice cream melt?

Materials change state as they heat up or cool down. Heating a solid above its melting point turns it to liquid. The melting point for ice cream is 0° Celsius.

To keep ice cream frozen solid, we store it in the freezer.

How does a liquid become a gas?

Heating a liquid to its boiling point turns it to a gas. The boiling point of water is 100° Celsius.

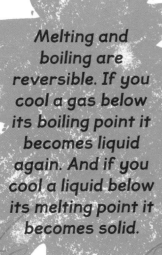

Melting and boiling are reversible. If you cool a gas below its boiling point it becomes liquid again. And if you cool a liquid below its melting point it becomes solid.

Not all things melt when heated – some just burn. Which of these things do you think would melt?

- Woolly sweater
- Egg
- Glass bottle
- Sausage
- Toffee
- Metal key
- Book
- Wooden chair

Answer:
glass, toffee and metal melt

A compendium of questions

Why is it cold at the North and South Poles?

The Earth is like a ball, so the top and bottom don't get much direct sunlight as they face away from the Sun.

Where do stars go in the daytime?

Nowhere! The light from the Sun is so bright that they just don't show up in daytime.

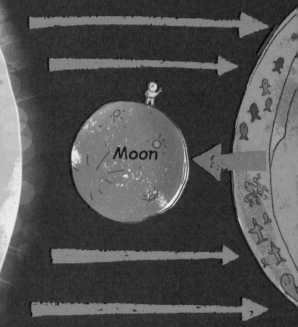

Moon

Why don't I freeze solid in icy weather?

You're warm-blooded, which means your body uses energy to keep you at a safe temperature.

What are shooting stars?

Meteorites – lumps of rock from space. They get so hot as they pass through the air above the Earth that they burn up, creating a streak of bright light.

Why does the tide go in and out?

The Moon's gravity pulls on the oceans. As the Earth turns, the water is pulled one way and then the other.

What is a cloud made of?

Tiny drops of water, so light that they are held up by the air. If too much water collects, the drops get heavier and fall as rain.

Why do I burp?

Food breaking down in your stomach makes gases. This collects in bubbles which come out at your top or bottom!

Why does a balloon go bang?

The air inside is under a lot of pressure. When the balloon bursts, air rushes out in a fast-moving wave. We hear this as a bang.

Is a bubble a solid, liquid or gas?

It is gas with a very thin skin of liquid around it.

Could astronauts go to the Sun?

No – the Sun is far too hot for any person or spaceship to survive getting close to.

Why are there no dinosaurs?

Dinosaurs and many other creatures all died out 65 million years ago by a natural disaster – probably a rock from space crashing into Earth.

At the South Pole, which way is up?

Towards the sky. Down is always towards the centre of the Earth. There is no up or down in space.

This way up!

Why isn't the world covered in poo?

Poo is eaten and broken down by dung beetles, worms and micro organisms. So poo is food for some things!

Can I be a scientist when I grow up?

Yes! Anyone can be a scientist — just stay curious!

41

If you could be any animal for a day, what would you be?

ANIMALS

Do you like warm weather better, or snow?

If you could eat one food every day what would it be?

What is an animal?

Animals are living things that do all of these things...

① Have babies

All animals can make new life like themselves — this is called **having babies**, or **reproduction**.

② Breathe

Animals **breathe** to take air into their bodies. The body needs a gas in the air called oxygen to keep working.

③ Use senses

An animal uses the **senses** of touch, taste, smell, sight and hearing to find out what is going on around it.

Those leaves look tasty!

④ Move

Most animals **move** to get to food and water, to find safe places, and to escape from danger.

> I learnt to stand up 30 minutes after I was born. How old were you when you learnt to stand?

⑤ Eat

Animals must **eat** food to stay alive. Food gives them energy so they can **move** and **grow**.

Munch!

⑥ Get rid of waste

Waste is leftover food that an animal's body doesn't need.

> Waste not want not! Dung beetles like me use elephant poo for lots of things!

⑦ Grow

All animals start small and **grow** bigger until they are old enough to **have babies** of their own.

Why do crocodiles eat stones?

Because they swallow their meaty meals whole, and the stones help to grind up the food in their tummies!

Crocs are one of the world's biggest carnivores, or meat-eaters. We eat fish, birds, rats, snakes, lizards and even deer and pigs.

What makes flamingos pink?

Flamingos are pink because they eat pink shrimps that live in VERY salty lakes! They feed with their heads upside down.

Can you see any other upside-down eaters around here?

Who likes eating greens?

Leaves and other greens taste great to herbivores (plant-eaters) like sloths. Some greens are tough to eat, so they spend lots of time chewing.

Anteaters like me eat ants and termites — thousands of them every day! We lick them up with our long, sticky tongues.

Are animals picky eaters?

They can be! Some only eat one special food. Others, like tiger sharks and brown bears, will eat almost anything they can find!

What are senses?

Senses are the body's way of finding out about the world. Animals use senses to locate food, find their way about, avoid danger and make friends. The five main senses are **hearing**, **sight**, **smell**, **taste** and **touch**.

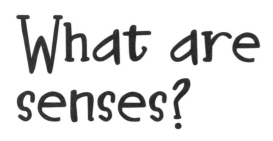

HEARING

Ear

Do bugs have ears?

Yes — lots of bugs can hear better than humans, but our ears can be in strange places! I'm a bush cricket, and my ears are on my legs.

What are whiskers for?

TOUCH

A cat's whiskers are super-sensitive. I use them to feel things — they can tell me if a space I want to crawl into is too small for my body.

How do snakes smell?

Snakes can smell with their tongues. They flick them in the air to detect any appealing pongs!

SMELL

TASTE

Why is it a bad idea to lick a frog?

I make a foul-tasting slime in my skin. It stops animals from eating me.

SIGHT

Do all animals have two eyes?

Some animals have more than two! Most spiders have eight eyes but cave spiders have none. They live in caves where it's always dark.

Did you know?

A **fulmar** is a foul seabird. It spits a stinky oil at anyone who gets too close.

The **giraffe** is the tallest animal that lives on land.

Lobsters have blue blood and some dogs have blue tongues.

When a **sandtiger shark** wants to sink to the seabed, it has to burp first!

A spiny **sea urchin** is covered in tiny feet. Its mouth is on its bottom!

Mimic octopuses can change shape and colour. They can pretend to be fish or sea snakes.

Sweat bees like the smell and taste of human sweat!

If a **sponge** is broken into bits, this strange sea creature is able to put itself back together again.

The **dung beetle** is the strongest animal on Earth. If it were the size of a human it could pull six buses full of people!

A **spider** eats about 2000 bugs a year.

Australian **burrowing frogs** cover themselves in slime, so when flies land on them they get stuck — and the frogs can gobble them up.

Bees waggle their bottoms in a crazy dance to tell each other where to find the best flowers.

Hippos don't just yawn when they are tired — they also yawn when they are angry or scared.

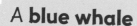

A **blue whale** eats millions of pink shrimps, so its poo is pink too. Each poo can be bigger than you!

A **catfish** can use its whole body to taste. Its skin is covered with taste buds.

What's inside an animal?

If you had to build an animal from scratch, here's what you would need...

Spine

① Framework

Most big animals have a **skeleton** – a framework of bones beneath their skin. Smaller animals have a tough outside – like a shell or strong skin – called an **exoskeleton**.

Ribs

③ Inner workings

Soft, squishy body parts called organs do useful jobs such as thinking, breathing and turning food into energy.

Brain

Tail

Lung

Liver

Heart

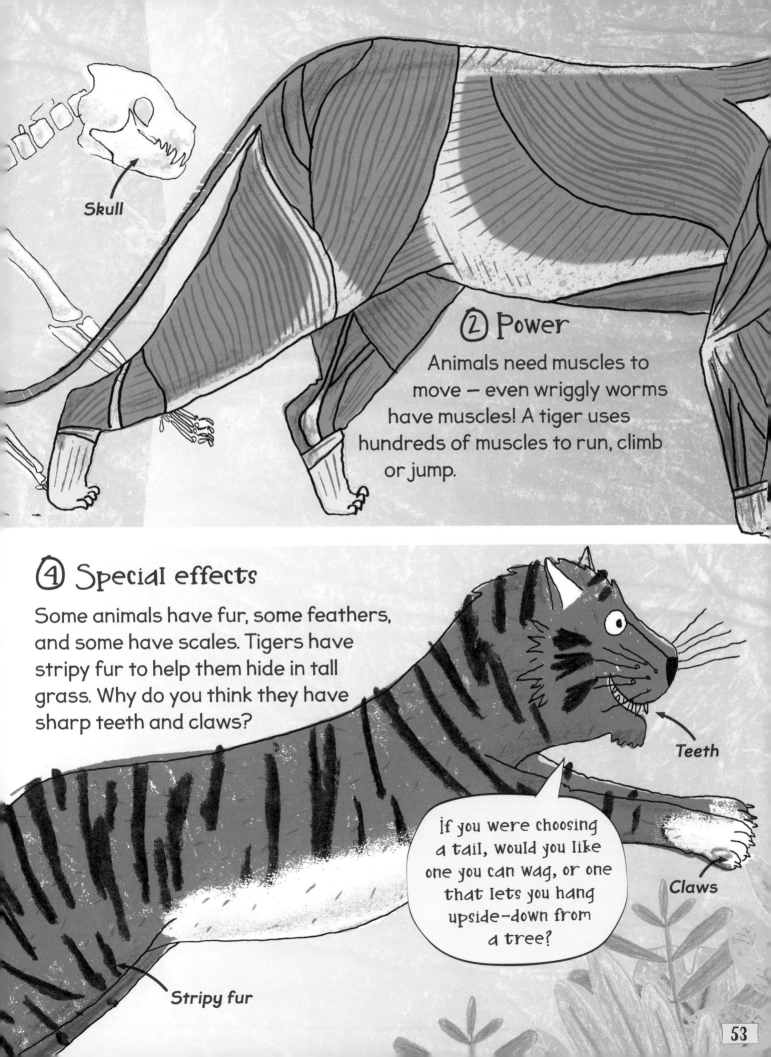

Skull

② Power

Animals need muscles to move – even wriggly worms have muscles! A tiger uses hundreds of muscles to run, climb or jump.

④ Special effects

Some animals have fur, some feathers, and some have scales. Tigers have stripy fur to help them hide in tall grass. Why do you think they have sharp teeth and claws?

Teeth

If you were choosing a tail, would you like one you can wag, or one that lets you hang upside-down from a tree?

Claws

Stripy fur

Why are you blue?

Colours and patterns make an animal beautiful! They can also make an animal look scary, or help it to hide.

Blue-ringed octopus

My colour is a sign of danger. When I'm scared, blue circles appear on my skin. They are a warning that I can kill any attackers with venom.

Blue morpho butterfly

Danger or disguise?

Some animals blend into the background. This is called camouflage. Others have colours and patterns that warn enemies to stay away. Which of these creatures are using camouflage, and which are using warning colours?

Strawberry poison dart frog

Pygmy seahorse

My colours help me hide. A blue or dark grey shark can prowl through the sea, unseen by the fish it is looking for.

Blue shark

Would you rather have blue feet, like me, or a blue bum, like a baboon?

Blue-footed booby

Southern crowned-pigeon

My beautiful blue feathers make me look healthy and fit to attract a mate.

Leaf insect

Banded sea krait

Lion

Would you rather?

Winter is coming! Would you prefer to travel to somewhere warm, like a **sand martin**, or curl up and sleep through it, like a **dormouse**?

Would you rather be spotted like a **leopard**, or striped like a **tiger**?

ZZzzz...

Is it better to have a long neck, like a **giraffe**...

...or lots of arms like an **octopus**?

You look soooo cute!

A giraffe uses its long neck to reach leaves in tall trees. An octopus uses its arms to move, touch, taste and gather food.

If you were an animal baby would you prefer to sit in dad's pouch, like a **seahorse**, or in mum's, like a **kangaroo**?

It's picnic time! Would you prefer to tuck into a rotting dead animal like a **vulture**, or suck down some animal poo like a **sea cucumber**?

Erm... yummy?

Would you rather have armour like a **pangolin**, or spikes like a **pufferfish**?

WHOOSH!

Would you rather be able to dive through the air at 200 kilometres an hour like a **peregrine falcon**, or fly 15,000 kilometres in a single journey like an **albatross**?

Is it better to be best friends with a **shark** or a **crocodile**?

Sharks and crocodiles are both big carnivores. That means they eat other animals, so it's probably not a good idea to try to make friends with either!

Will you play with me?

Why do spiders do cartwheels?

TUMBLE

Desert spiders that have to get across hot sand do cartwheels so their feet don't get burnt!

How high can you jump?

BOUNCE

LEAP

Kangaroos can jump up to 3 metres into the air, but we can't walk, or move backwards.

Why do orangutans have long arms?

Long arms are great for swinging through trees. We also have hands for gripping branches and grabbing fruit.

SWING

HOVER

Antelopes leap several metres at a time, springing up in the air to escape from danger.

Which bird flies, but goes nowhere?

A hummingbird does. It flaps and twists its wings so that it can hover in front of a flower, where it drinks the sweet nectar.

I can leap more than 100 times my own height.

SPRING

Fleas jump so they can leap from animal to animal, where they suck blood!

How fast do cheetahs sprint?

A cheetah is the fastest running animal on the planet. It can reach top speeds of up to 100 kilometres an hour.

① Built for speed

A cheetah's body is packed with small but powerful muscles.

Why do cheetahs run fast?

Like many hunters, cheetahs turn on the speed when they want to catch their lunch! The antelope they chase need to be fast too, if they hope to escape.

Why are tortoises so slow?

Tortoises plod along slowly because they don't need speed to catch their lunch – they eat grass! They don't need to be fast to escape from danger either because their tough shells protect them like a suit of armour.

② Big strides

It has a super-bendy spine and long, slim legs.

③ Long leap

All four of a cheetah's feet leave the ground as it runs.

Why do crabs run sideways?
Because the way their legs bend means they can't run forwards!

Who's playing statues?
During the day, a potoo bird doesn't move at all! It pretends to be a branch. At night, it flies about, hunting bugs to eat.

How many?

An octopus has **3** hearts but an earthworm has **5**.

A squid has **2** tentacles...

... and it has **8** arms.

Sea otters have **800 million** hairs on their bodies.

Tree kangaroos can jump **30** metres from a tree to the ground below.

A snow leopard can leap more than **10** metres in a single bound.

A snake can live for up to **6** months without eating

A giraffe's tongue is **45** centimetres long.

20 The number of hours three-toed sloths, koalas and lions might sleep in one day.

500,000

The number of kilometres a sooty tern can fly without stopping for a rest.

Monarch butterflies can go on incredible journeys – one butterfly flew more than **4000** kilometres to lay its eggs!

4

The number of wings a bee has.

1

The number of hours it takes a snail to slime its way along just **1** metre of ground.

750

The largest number of legs ever counted on a millipede.

A mother cane toad can lay **35,000** eggs at a time.

36

The length, in centimetres, of the longest insect – a type of stick insect called Chan's megastick.

Is anyone at home?

Yes! An animal's home is a safe place where it can look after its babies. Animal homes are called habitats. They can be as big as an ocean or as small as a single leaf.

Froghopper nest

Who lives in a home made of spit?

Young froghopper insects build a home of froth around themselves! This 'spit' keeps them safe while they grow.

Why do frogs like water?

Because they need to lay their eggs in it. They are amphibians, which means they can live in water or on land.

Some animals that live in or near water have to come up to the surface to breathe air.

Others have gills and breathe underwater.

Frogs like to live in wet places

Can animals make things?

Yes, some animals are expert builders and can make super structures.

① *A hoop of grass...*
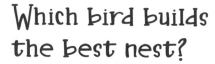

Which bird builds the best nest?

② *...turns into a ball...*

③ *...and then a home.*

A dad weaver bird makes his nest by stitching blades of grass together, then stuffing feathers inside to make a soft bed. He sings to tell mum she can lay her eggs there.

① **Strong silk makes the frame**

Why do spiders build webs?

So they can trap flies. A spider makes the silk in its body and then spins it into a web.

② **Sticky silk is used in the spiral**

Who loves mud?

Millions of termites do! They build their huge towering homes from mud. A group of termites that live together is called a colony, and their home can last for years.

There are passages, tunnels, and places to store food inside

A termite mound can be more than 2 metres high!

HOME SWEET HOME

A single queen lays all the eggs

What's the point of mums and dads?

Some animal babies look after themselves, but many need mums and dads to give them food and keep them safe.

Where do penguins keep their eggs?

Emperor penguins like us keep our eggs off the ice by holding them on our feet. The skin on our tummies is covered with fluffy feathers to keep our chicks warm.

How does a baby orca sleep?

Baby orcas can swim as soon as they are born, and they sleep while they are swimming! Orcas can rest one half of their brain at a time. The other half stays wide-awake.

A baby orca is called a calf

Do baby animals drink milk?

Yes, furry animals are called mammals and they feed their babies with milk. A polar bear mum looks after her cubs in a snowy den during the long, cold winter.

ZZZZZZ

Would you rather have an orca, a penguin or a polar bear for a parent?

A compendium of questions

Are sharks the most dangerous animals?

Sharks don't usually attack people. Snakes, donkeys and dogs hurt people more often than sharks!

I'm harmless to humans! I love to eat small fish, squid and jellyfish.

How does a squid escape from a hungry shark?

A squid squirts jets of water, and zooms off! The jets of water push the squid forward. This is called jet propulsion.

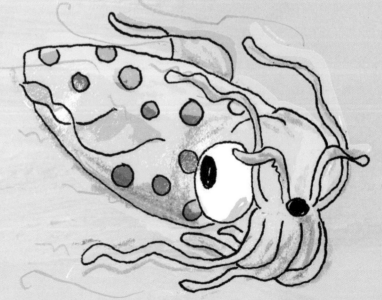

Can a lizard run across water?

A basilisk lizard can. It runs really fast and uses its big feet and tail to help it balance on top of the water.

Whip-like tail

Long toes

Why do jellyfish wobble?

Jellyfish don't have any bones and their bodies are full of water, like real jelly!

Do all animals have bones?

Mammals, birds, reptiles, amphibians and fish have bones. All other animals — including bugs, crabs and octopuses — don't.

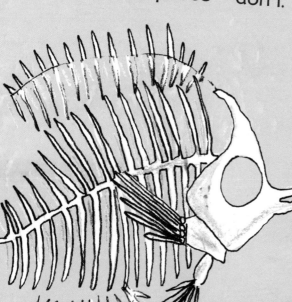

What is venom?

Venom is a poison. Venomous animals can inject it using their fangs, claws, spines or stings. They use it to defend themselves, or to kill animals for food.

Is a bat a bird?

No, it's a flying mammal. Bats are the only mammals that fly.

Do lions purr?

Big cats roar but can't purr, and small cats purr but can't roar. Big cats sometimes make a noise like a growly purr!

I'm safer from attack in the air than I would be running along the ground.

Do camels keep water in their humps?

No — a camel's hump is full of fat, not water.

The gliding lizard uses its long tail to steer through the air

How do animals glide?

Gliding lizards, frogs and squirrels have large flaps of skin that they stretch out before they leap from a tree. The skin works like a parachute to help them glide, and land softly.

What's the smallest bird?

A bee hummingbird. It's smaller than your thumb. An ostrich is the biggest bird.

How many animals are in the world?

No one knows, but there are billions of ants, so it must be lots!

What colour are your eyes?

If you could have an extra sense, what would it be?

MY BODY

Do you go to bed early or late?

How tall are you?

What is my body for?

Your body lets you see, hear, smell, taste and touch the world around you. You can use it to run, jump, think, talk, and have all kinds of fun. Without it, you couldn't do anything.

Our bodies look different on the outside, but inside we all have bones, muscles and blood.

Cells make up tissue such as bone, muscle and blood.

Why are cells so special?

Because they are the tiny building blocks that together make up your body. Different cells do different jobs. You have blood cells, bone cells, skin cells and lots more.

Bone cells make up your skeleton

How can doctors see inside our bodies?

Doctors can look inside the body with scans and X-rays to see where all the parts are and how they fit together. They can even look at single cells with microscopes that magnify them.

X-rays can check for broken bones.

Muscle cells help to form every muscle in your body

Your blood contains trillions of red blood cells

Why do I need to eat?

Food provides the energy your body needs to keep working. Chemicals from food repair your body and help it grow. Your body breaks down food and rearranges the chemicals to make skin, hair, bones and all the other parts.

Can i balance my food?

Yes you can, but not on your head! It's important to eat a wide range of foods from different food groups to make sure you stay fit and healthy.

Fruit and vegetables
Eat lots of these for fibre and goodness

Protein
Meat, fish and beans help your body grow and repair itself

Why is water so important?

About 60 percent of your body is water — it's in every cell. But you lose water when you pee and sweat, and every time you breathe out. You need to drink to replace the water you lose.

What happens when I eat?

The food you eat takes a long and twisty route through your digestive system. At each stage, your body pulls out the good things it needs.

Always wash your hands before eating.

① How do teeth help?

Your teeth break up food as you chew. They chew it into smaller pieces and mash it around. Food mixes with saliva in your mouth, making it easier to swallow.

② Where does food go first?

When you swallow, food goes into a tube in your throat called your oesophagus (say 'ee-sof-a-guss'). Muscles push the food down to your stomach, squeezing behind the lump of food so that it moves along.

From mouth to stomach takes 5–8 seconds

Oesophagus

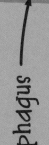

⑤ Why do I need to poo?

To get rid of the bits that your body doesn't need. These parts are squashed together and mixed with dead cells and water from your gut. They leave your body when you go to the toilet.

Always wash your hands after going to the toilet.

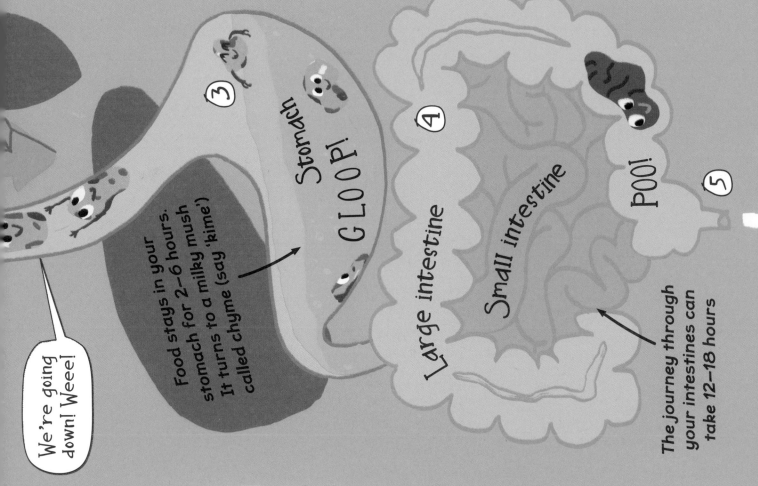

We're going down! Weee!

Food stays in your stomach for 2–6 hours. It turns to a milky mush called chyme (say 'kime')

③

Stomach
GLOOP!

④ Large intestine

Small intestine

POO!

⑤

The journey through your intestines can take 12–18 hours

③ Why is there acid in my stomach?

Acid dissolves food into a gloopy liquid. Muscles in your stomach also churn the mixture around to break it up.

④ What goes on in my intestines?

A milky mushy liquid moves into and through your intestines where nutrients (useful chemicals) and water are absorbed. The leftover parts are turned into... poo!

How many?

35 The number of tonnes of food the average person eats in their life.

110,000 The number of hairs on the head of a dark-haired person; blondes have more and redheads have fewer.

37 trillion The number of human cells in an adult body.

1.5–2 The area in square metres of an adult's skin.

0.5 The volume of gas in litres that your gut produces each day.

Your nose can detect **1 trillion** smells.

69 The largest number of babies anyone has had.

16 The speed in kilometres per hour of a sneeze.

A hair grows **1.25** centimetres each month.

900 The length in centimetres of the longest-ever fingernail.

120 The speed in metres per second of a message travelling along a nerve.

5 The amount in litres of blood in an average adult human.

3 The length in millimetres of your smallest bone (it's inside your ear).

What is my skeleton made of?

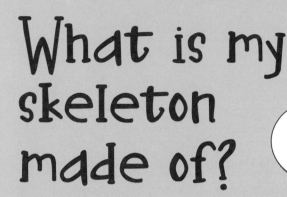

Imagine how floppy and blobby you'd be without bones!

Bones form the rigid framework for your body – your skeleton. They support your body and provide somewhere for your muscles to fix to.

Skull

Clavicle

Jaw

Humerus

Ribs

Sternum

Spine

Ulna

Radius

Pelvis

Femur

Patella

How do muscles move me?

Most muscles are fixed to your bones. As they contract, they pull the bones along with them, moving your body. Being active makes your muscles strong. Run, swim, jump, cycle – do anything you like!

Biceps muscle contracts to bend your arm

contract

relax

Fibula

Tibia

Tendon attaches muscle to bone

Triceps muscle relaxes

Phalanges

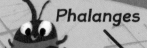

Which muscle works the hardest?

Your heart works harder than any other muscle. It never stops pumping blood around your body throughout your life.

I need exercise too! It helps to make me strong.

Knee joint

Ankle joint

Activities like dancing are good for getting your heart working.

Hip joint

Joints make you flexible, you couldn't move without them.

Elbow joint

Wrist joint

How does my body bend?

You have lots of joints in your body such as in your knees, elbows, shoulders, ankles and wrists. These are places where bones meet, and they allow your body to bend or move in different ways.

Activities like swimming make you breathe fast

Lung

Heart

Lung

What happens when I breathe?

When you breathe in, your lungs fill with air. Oxygen from the air goes into your blood and is delivered to your whole body. Old air is pushed out when you breathe out.

How does my blood deliver oxygen?

Your blood flows through tubes called blood vessels. These reach every single part of your body to make sure you have all the oxygen you need. Your heart and blood together are called the circulatory system.

Blood vessels

Why does my heart thump?

When you exercise, your heart beats faster to pump blood around your body quickly, to deliver the oxygen your muscles need. You also breathe faster to get more oxygen, and you feel out of breath.

Why can't I breathe underwater?

Because you don't have gills like a fish! Your lungs can only take oxygen from the air. A fish's gills can take dissolved oxygen from water. When you swim underwater, you need to come to the surface for air.

Why am I ticklish?

Because you have a sense of touch! Your body uses five senses to find out about the world around you. Your senses pick up information and send it to your brain.

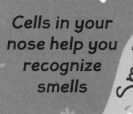

Cells in your nose help you recognize smells

Smell

Eyes let in light to help you see all around you

See

Ears pick up sound vibrations to help you hear

Hear

Special areas on your tongue tell you what something tastes like

Touch

Skin is packed with touch sensors to help you feel

Taste

Why can't I see in the dark?

Because you need light to bounce off objects and into your eyes. A lens in your eye helps focus the light, and a nerve carries information to your brain to make an image — and that is what you see.

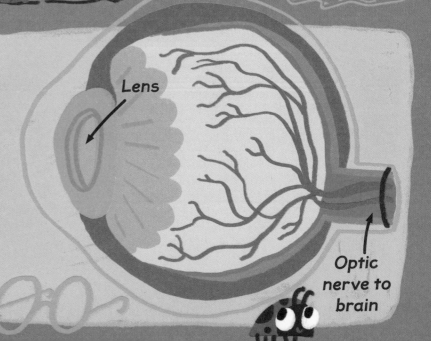

Lens

Optic nerve to brain

Why are ears a funny shape?

The shape of your ears helps to funnel sound into them. Sound is then carried inside your ear, where signals are sent along a nerve to your brain, so it can make sense of what you hear.

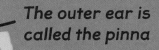

The outer ear is called the pinna

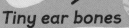

Soundwaves in

Tiny ear bones

Auditory nerve to brain

How do I smell?

Your sense of smell is produced by cells high above and behind your nose. Tiny particles of the thing you are smelling reach those cells.

Tiny cells detect smell particles and send signals to your brain

Smell particles go up your nose

What helps me taste food?

Your tongue is covered with blobs surrounded by tiny taste buds. The taste buds send messages to your brain about the chemicals dissolved in food, and your brain turns the information into tastes.

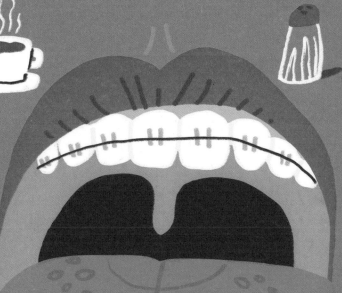

Did you know?

Your **teeth** are as strong as a **shark's** teeth – but your jaws are smaller so you can't bite like a shark.

Babies can hear before they're born, though sounds from the outside are a bit **muffled**.

I hope I grow up to be a better singer than Mum.

An **adult** can survive three weeks without **food**, but only about four days without **water**.

Your **ears** are important to your sense of **balance**.

In **complete darkness,** your eyes could spot the light from a candle 48 kilometres away.

Some parts of your body are never replaced. The **enamel** on your teeth and the **goo** inside your **eyes** have to last a lifetime.

By the time you were six months old, your **eyes** were already **two thirds** their adult size.

A C P X B

Hi. Hi Hi Hi Hi

Children can hear higher sounds than adults, including **bats** squeaking and **ultrasonic** dog whistles.

Fingerprints are not the body's only unique pattern. You can also be identified by your **tongue print**, your personal **smell** and the pattern in your **iris** (the coloured part of your eye).

Your **blood** is made inside your **bones**.

Is my brain in charge?

What you say, think and how you move, and everything else you do, is controlled by your brain.

Stand on one foot and spin the ball.

It receives information

A network of nerves tells your brain what is happening to your body. Your brain is linked to your body by your spinal cord

Brain

Spinal cord

It sends messages

Your brain sends messages to your body, telling it how to react or move

Nerve network

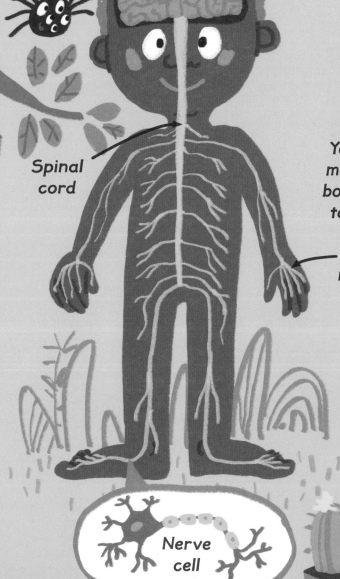

Nerve cell

What do my nerves do?

Nerves are collections of nerve cells (neurons). They carry information between all parts of your body and brain. When you see, smell, taste or hear anything, information is carried by nerves to your brain super-quickly.

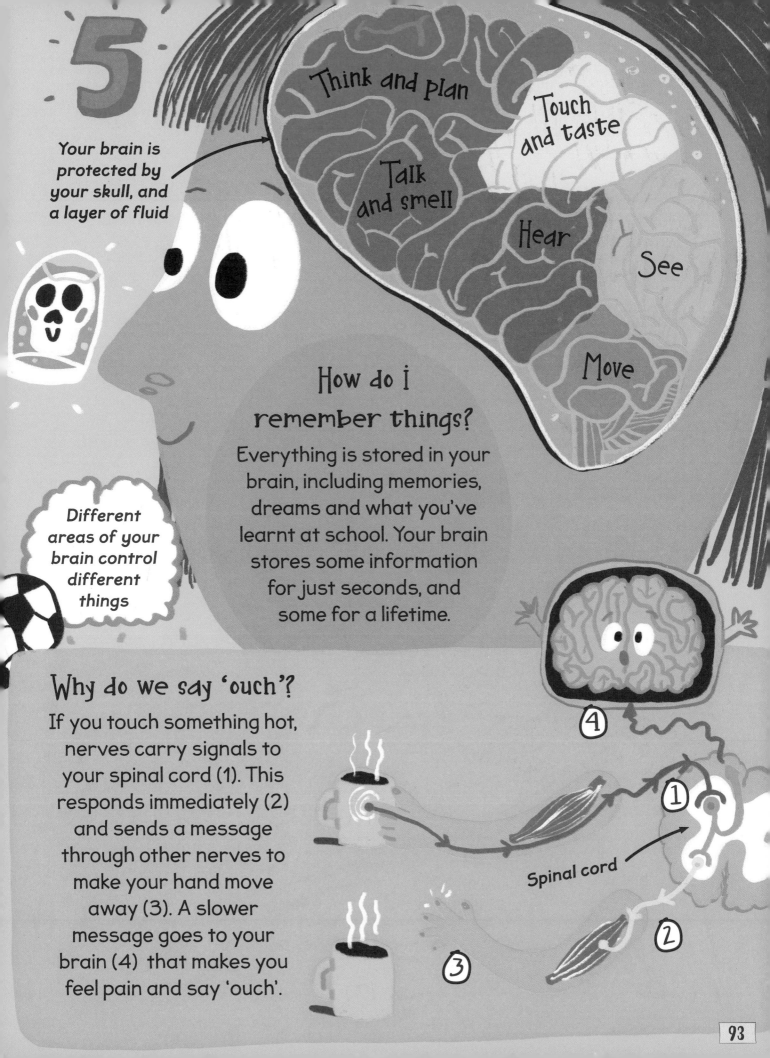

5

Your brain is protected by your skull, and a layer of fluid

Think and plan

Touch and taste

Talk and smell

Hear

See

Move

Different areas of your brain control different things

How do I remember things?

Everything is stored in your brain, including memories, dreams and what you've learnt at school. Your brain stores some information for just seconds, and some for a lifetime.

Why do we say 'ouch'?

If you touch something hot, nerves carry signals to your spinal cord (1). This responds immediately (2) and sends a message through other nerves to make your hand move away (3). A slower message goes to your brain (4) that makes you feel pain and say 'ouch'.

④

①

Spinal cord

②

③

93

Why do I sleep?

Your body uses the time you're asleep to repair any injuries, grow, rest and sort out what you've experienced and learnt during the day. No one knows exactly how sleep works, but we do know that we can't live without it.

Does everyone dream?

Yes, but not everyone remembers their dreams. Most people have 3–5 dreams each night. Even cats and dogs have dreams!

No one knows what animals dream about!

Why are dreams so weird?

As your brain sorts through information while you sleep, it's in a jumbled order, with recent events mixed up with old memories. Some people think secret meanings are hidden in dreams.

Each dream can last 20 minutes or a few seconds

How much sleep do I need?

We need different amounts of sleep at different ages. Newborn babies sleep for a long time every day. Adults sleep less.

Would you rather?

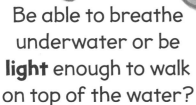

Be able to breathe underwater or be **light** enough to walk on top of the water?

Have a really long **tongue** or really long **fingers**?

Have **super-keen sight** or be able to hear very **quiet sounds** like ants munching their food?

Grow really long **fingernails** or really **long hair**?

Have **unbreakable** bones or **uncuttable** skin?

Have **wings** or a **tail**?

Be **wobbly** like a jellyfish with no bones, or have a **hard** outer shell like a tortoise?

Be entirely **furry** or entirely **bald**?

Have eyes in the back of your **head** or in the tips of your **fingers**?

Be able to run really **fast** or for a really **long** time?

Where do babies come from?

Babies come from inside their mum's body. A baby grows in the mum's uterus, where it gets everything it needs until it's ready to be born.

I can feel the baby kicking!

Goodness from the mother's food is carried along the cord to the baby

Egg cell divides again and again

Day 1

Day 2

Days 3–4

Cord

Uterus

How fast does a baby grow?

Inside its mum, a baby grows really fast. It starts off as a tiny egg, which divides to make the billions of cells that make up the whole baby. After nine months, the baby is big enough to be born.

12 weeks
5 centimetres

20 weeks
16 centimetres

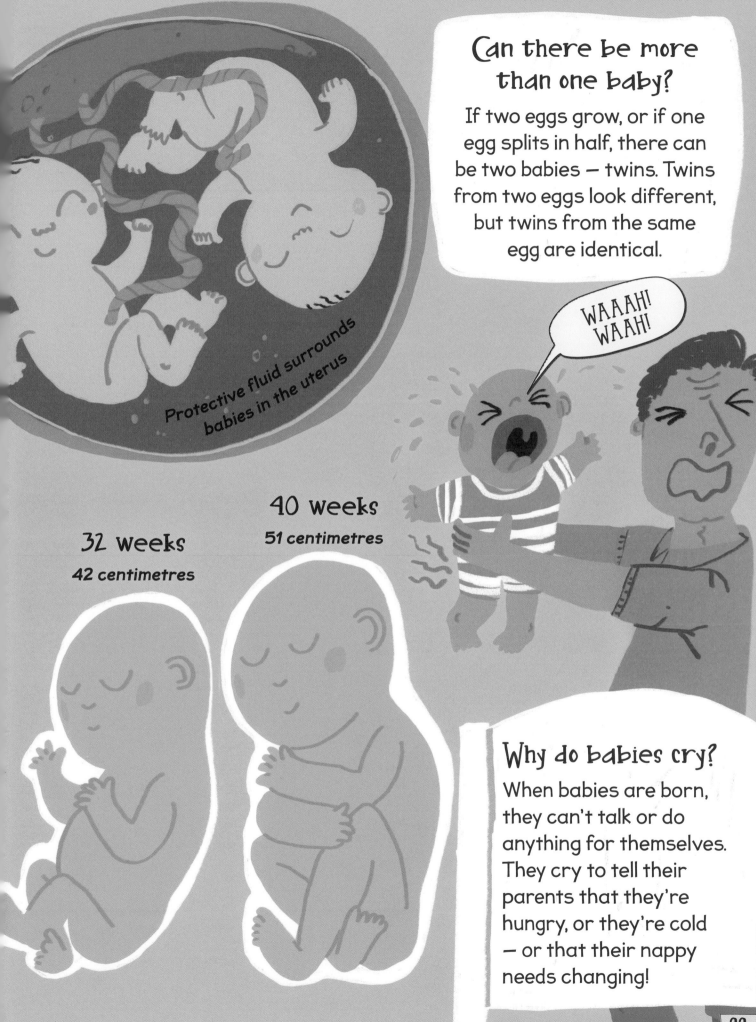

Can there be more than one baby?

If two eggs grow, or if one egg splits in half, there can be two babies – twins. Twins from two eggs look different, but twins from the same egg are identical.

Protective fluid surrounds babies in the uterus

WAAAH! WAAH!

40 weeks
51 centimetres

32 weeks
42 centimetres

Why do babies cry?

When babies are born, they can't talk or do anything for themselves. They cry to tell their parents that they're hungry, or they're cold – or that their nappy needs changing!

Am i always growing?

You keep growing from when you are born until your late teens or early twenties. But the speed you grow at slows down. A baby triples its weight in a year.

Do you know how tall you are?

Babies double their weight in five months. If you kept doing that you'd be huge!

5 years

6 months

10 years

Newborn

How do i get taller?

A soft, flexible substance called cartilage grows inside your bones, making them longer. The cartilage slowly hardens into bone.

Cartilage hardens to bone

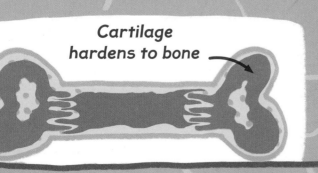

Why does my hair need cutting?

Your hair grows throughout your life, so you have to keep cutting it. Hair grows from a little pit on your scalp called a hair follicle, but the hair you can see is actually dead. That's why it doesn't hurt to have a haircut.

Hair follicle

15 years

20 years

70 years

Your ears keep getting bigger too, but very slowly.

Grandma? Grandpa?

Do we shrink as we get older?

Yes! The bones of the spine get squashed closer together over the years. Some older people also get a curved spine and stoop, and that makes them look even shorter.

A compendium of questions

What are goosebumps?

They are bumps on your skin where tiny muscles make your hairs stand up if you are cold or scared.

Why do my first teeth fall out?

Your first teeth are temporary — you have them until your mouth grows large enough for your permanent teeth. You have 20 first teeth, and they are replaced by larger, stronger, teeth.

Your permanent teeth need to last your whole life, so it's important to look after them!

What are hiccups?

If the muscle across your chest suddenly squeezes, it can snap shut the opening to your vocal flaps, making the 'hic' sound.

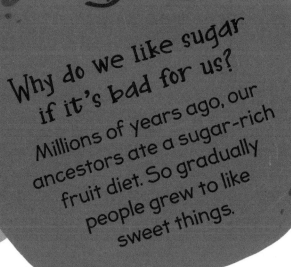

Why do we like sugar if it's bad for us?

Millions of years ago, our ancestors ate a sugar-rich fruit diet. So gradually people grew to like sweet things.

Why do I yawn?

No one's quite sure, but possibly as a way of getting more oxygen into your body quickly.

Why do we get wrinkles?

As skin ages, it loses its elasticity, so it can't spring back into shape after stretching (such as when you smile).

Why don't I have to remember to breathe?

Why is blood red?

Blood contains a chemical for carrying oxygen that contains iron. When this chemical picks up oxygen, it turns redder.

My knee hurts now, but soon I'll have a scab!

What makes a scab?

When your blood meets the air, special cells called platelets break up and mix with a protein in blood to make tangly fibres, forming a scab.

Your brain deals with all kinds of automatic activities without you having to think about them, including breathing, and digesting food.

What is my tummy button for?

When you were inside your mother, you got nutrients and oxygen through the umbilical cord that connected you to her body. The tummy button is what's left after the cord is cut.

Why do I sleep more when I'm ill?

Your body needs energy to fight the illness, so to save energy it makes you sleep.

Have you ever grown a plant from a seed?

If you could be friends with a bat or a bee, which would you choose?

PLANTS

Would you rather be a caterpillar or a butterfly?

What's your favourite fruit or vegetable?

What is a plant?

Plants are living things that can...

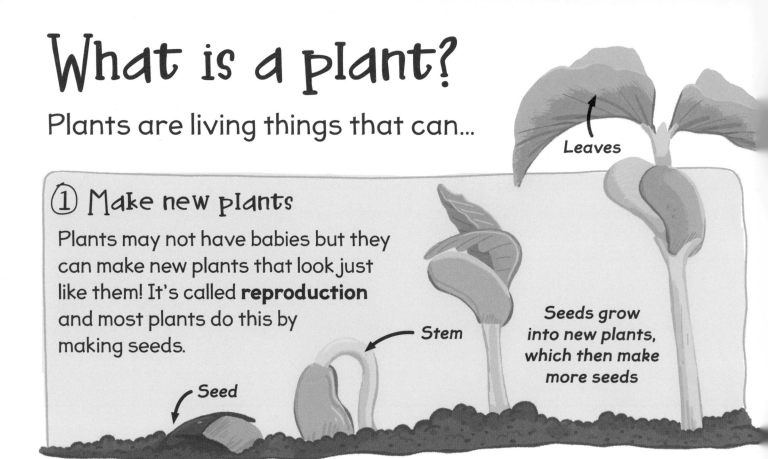

Leaves

① Make new plants

Plants may not have babies but they can make new plants that look just like them! It's called **reproduction** and most plants do this by making seeds.

Stem

Seed

Seeds grow into new plants, which then make more seeds

② Breathe

Plants **breathe** air through tiny holes in their leaves.

We breathe in carbon dioxide from the air and breathe out oxygen.

③ Get rid of waste

Plants are brilliant because when they breathe they make a **waste** gas called oxygen — it's the gas we need to stay alive!

Thanks for giving me clean air to breathe!

④ Use senses

A plant may not have eyes but it can sense light and it can feel, smell, hear and...

⑤ ...move

Plants **move** their leaves to face the Sun. Seeds **travel** too. Some of them are carried a long way on the wind.

I'm off to find a great place to grow into a new plant!

⑥ Get food

Some plants eat bugs, but most of them make their own **food**. They use this to...

I'm a sticky sundew plant catching insects for my dinner!

From little acorns...

...mighty oaks can grow.

⑦ ...grow

Most plants – even giant trees – start their lives as seeds, but they soon grow and change.

Do plants get hungry?

Plants don't feel hungry the same way that animals do, but they do need food. Animals eat their food, but plants make all the food they need.

I can store the food I make in different parts of me and save it for the winter.

Sunlight

Flowering plant

Flower

Leaf

Stem

Oxygen out

Carbon dioxide in

Plants use sunlight to turn water and carbon dioxide from the air into food. This is called photosynthesis.

Why are leaves green?

Because they have a green substance called chlorophyll inside them. This helps the plant collect the energy from sunlight and turn it into food.

Water is sucked up from the soil by a plant's roots

Roots also suck up minerals to help a plant grow

How do plants feed the world?

Plants are the beginning of most food chains. This is when living things depend on each other for food. Animals eat plants — fruits, vegetables, nuts and seeds — and some animals also eat other animals.

A food chain shows how energy and nutrients pass from one living thing to another.

I turn the Sun's energy into my food.

I get my energy from eating plants.

Eating small animals and plants gives me the energy to run and play.

Winter

Spring

Autumn

Summer

Why do plants lose their leaves?

In the autumn many leaves change colour and fall off. This is so the plant can store up water and energy over the winter, ready to grow new leaves in the spring.

Did you know?

Plants are cool! When they absorb **sunlight** to make their food they make the air cooler. This helps to control the Earth's temperature.

Solar panels work just like **leaves** because they collect energy from sunlight. We use that energy to make electricity.

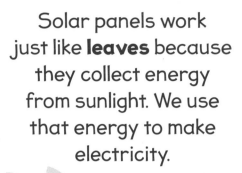

Nutrients are the foods, minerals and vitamins we need to live and grow.

Mimosa plants are shy! If something touches them they quickly fold up their leaves. It's a clever way to avoid being eaten.

Eating **bananas** can make you happy! They contain nutrients that help you to feel good and sleep well.

Yuk!

Argh!

When some plants hear the sound of **caterpillars** munching nearby they make nasty tasting chemicals so the caterpillars leave them alone!

The largest leaves belong to **arum plants**. Some have heart-shaped leaves that grow more than 3 metres wide.

Just one **elephant** eats 200 kilograms of plant food every day.

I'm a Japanese morning glory and I change from purple to blue throughout the day.

Some flowers get a suntan! They **change colour** through the day as they warm up.

Mmm, you smell nice. I'm going to wrap myself around you.

Plants don't have noses but some of them can smell. **Dodder plants** grow on other plants. They sniff out their favourites and grow towards them!

Which plants snap, munch and stick?

Yum!

Some plants don't just make food from sunlight. They eat things too! They are called carnivorous, or meat-eating, plants.

> We live in dark, boggy places where there's not much sunlight to help make our food, so we eat small creatures to survive.

How do plants catch bugs?

Venus flytraps have trap-shaped leaves coated in hairs. When a spider, beetle or fly crawls over the hairs, the plant's trap snaps shut! The bug tries to escape, but there is no way out.

Snap!

Venus flytrap

Which plants drown their food?

Pitcher plants grow jug-shaped leaves that fill with water. Small creatures are tempted by the plant's smell and fall in, often drowning in the liquid at the bottom of the 'jug'.

Some pitcher plants are big enough to catch frogs and mice!

Pitcher plant

Stick!

Which plants trap with glue?

Sundew Plant

Once i trap my prey, i make liquid that dissolves the bug into a gloopy soup.

Sundew plants have delicious-looking red droplets that attract passing bugs. They are actually sticky glue, and when a bug lands on them it sticks. The plant then folds over and begins to dissolve the bug. Yum!

Why are flowers pretty?

Flowers have a very important job to do – it's called pollination – and many of them need insects to help. Colours, smells and shapes of flowers attract insects to a plant to pollinate it.

Pollen grows on stamens – the male parts of a flower

Pollen lands here and grows a tube down to the ovary to make new seeds

Colourful petals attract insects

Pollen grains are tiny and look like yellow or orange dust

What is pollination?

Plants make pollen. It comes from the male part of a flower and joins with a flower's egg to make a new plant seed. Insects carry pollen from one flower to another flower's eggs. This is called pollination.

Flowers make nectar at the bottom of petals. It's a sugary liquid that bugs love!

Eggs are inside a flower's ovary. This is the female part of a flower

Why do bees have baskets?

Some bees have special pouches on their legs that they use as baskets to carry the pollen they collect from flowers.

I gather pollen from flowers to use as food in my bee colony.

Bee

Pollen

Banana flower

Bat

Why do bananas need bats?

Banana, cocoa and mango plants are pollinated by bats. They visit the flowers to drink nectar, get covered in pollen and carry it from plant to plant. Birds and moths also pollinate some plants.

I smell sweet at night to tempt moths to come and pollinate me.

Moth

Honeysuckle

How many?

1

The number of days it takes a swarm of locusts to munch through 190,000 tonnes of plants.

2000

The age in years of an ancient seed found by scientists. They planted it and it grew into a healthy magnolia tree!

The world's tallest flowering plant is a eucalyptus tree called Centurion that grows in Australia. It's **100** metres tall!

It takes just **1/50th** of a second for the bladderwort pond plant to catch mosquito larvae in its traps.

I am the fastest killer in the plant kingdom!

150 years old — the age of a giant bromeliad before it grows its first flower. It dies afterwards.

It can take **10** days for a Venus flytrap to digest a dead bug.

A saguaro cactus grows just **4** centimetres in ten years, but bamboo can grow **90** centimetres in a single day!

200

The number of litres of water one corn plant needs to grow. That's more than two full bathtubs!

500 different types of plant are pollinated by bats.

There are **12,500** different types of tree growing in the Amazon rainforest.

Why are tomatoes red?

Tomatoes and other fruits are colourful to tell animals that they are ripe and ready to eat.

I'm tiny and green because I'm not ready to eat!

I'm red, plump, juicy and sweet. Eat me!

Tomato plant

Fruits have seeds in them. When animals eat the fruits, and then do a poo, they spread the seeds to new places where they grow into new plants.

Apple

Seeds

Warning!

Only eat fruits and nuts you have been told are safe to eat.

Why do fruits grow?

When a plant grows some new seeds, the fruit of the plant grows around the seeds to protect them.

Can seeds grow inside me?

Seeds can't grow inside animals or people. They need soil, water and oxygen to start growing.

Water goes into the seed and it swells

There is food in the seed for the new plant

Squirrel

Agouti

Why are nuts hard?

Nuts are hard fruits. They are hard to protect the seeds inside, or to help them move safely to new places.

I'm the only animal with teeth strong enough to break open a Brazil nut pod to reach the nuts inside.

I bury acorns so I can eat them in winter. If I forget where I put them they can grow into oak trees!

Have you ever tried to grow a seed? It's easy peasy!

The seedling has a shoot and little leaves

Pea plant

The new plant starts to grow

Roots grow into the soil to collect more water and stop the plant from blowing away

Did Diplodocus eat flowers?

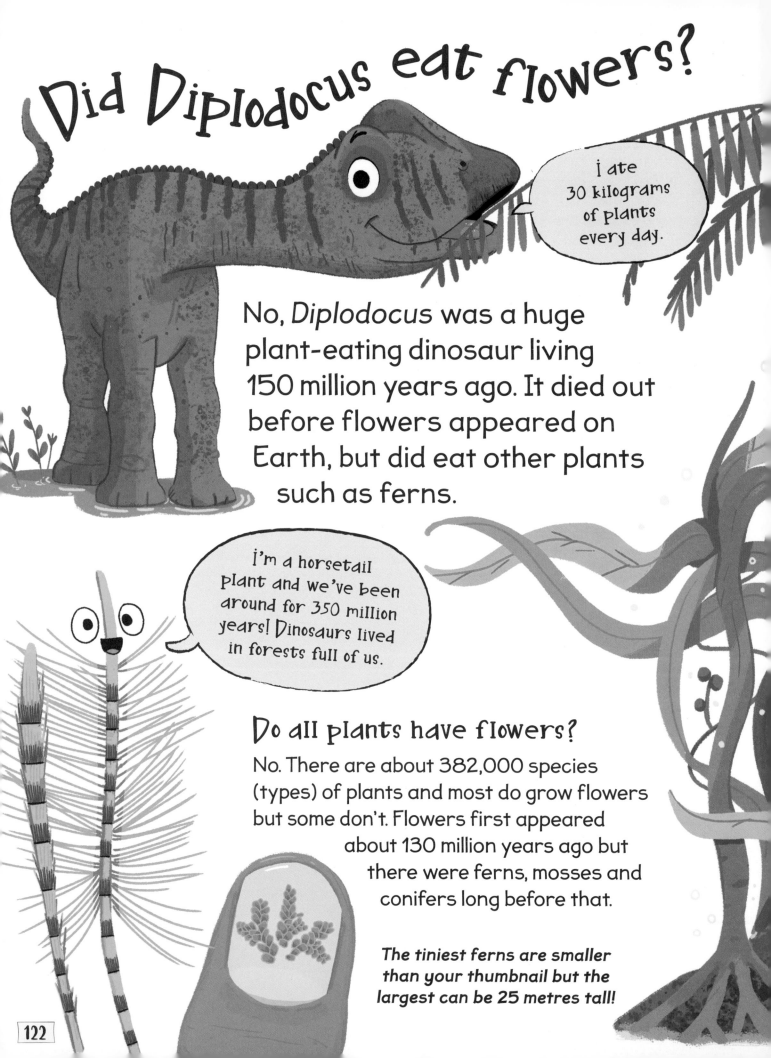

I ate 30 kilograms of plants every day.

No, *Diplodocus* was a huge plant-eating dinosaur living 150 million years ago. It died out before flowers appeared on Earth, but did eat other plants such as ferns.

I'm a horsetail plant and we've been around for 350 million years! Dinosaurs lived in forests full of us.

Do all plants have flowers?

No. There are about 382,000 species (types) of plants and most do grow flowers but some don't. Flowers first appeared about 130 million years ago but there were ferns, mosses and conifers long before that.

The tiniest ferns are smaller than your thumbnail but the largest can be 25 metres tall!

What is an evergreen?

It's a plant that keeps its leaves all year round. Conifers are evergreen trees that are often triangular — the perfect shape for growing in snowy places, as snow slips right off the branches without snapping them!

Conifers grow their seeds inside cones instead of in flowers or fruits

Pine trees, redwoods and fir trees are all types of conifer.

Kelp use sticky pads to fix themselves to the rocks or the seabed.

Can plants grow in the sea?

Yes! Seaweeds belong to a group of plants called algae. Giant kelp is the world's biggest seaweed and it grows in undersea forests. A single strand of kelp can grow to 30 metres long!

How do plants stay safe?

Many animals eat plants, and that's not good news for our green friends! They need to defend themselves from attack and some use prickly thorns and poisons to do this.

Spiky thorns!

Deadly nightshade

Who hugs trees to death?

i do! i'm a strangler fig. i wrap myself around a tall tree to hold me up. Eventually, the tree dies, but i survive!

Strangler fig

Warning!

Only eat berries you have been told are safe to eat.

Why are some berries deadly?

Berries often look tasty, but some contain poison to put animals off eating them. Deadly nightshade and foxglove plants can stop your heart from beating, but doctors can also make medicines from them.

Cactus

My fat stem stores water as it rarely rains in a desert. I'm covered in needle-like leaves called spines.

I'm a prickly sweet chestnut. My case only cracks open when the nuts inside are ripe to be eaten by animals who then spread my seeds far and wide.

What's the point of thorns and prickles?

Many plants have sharp thorns and prickles to stop animals from eating them.

Sweet chestnut

We are soft, juicy and tasty, so many animals would like to eat us – but we have a surprise for them!

Nettle

Ouch!

Why do nettles sting?

Nettles have tiny stinging hairs, each with a bead of acid on its tip. If you touch a nettle the hairs prick your skin and the beads release the acid.

Would you rather?

Would you rather sit under a **palm tree** where coconuts might fall on your head, or swim through the roots of a **mangrove tree** where young crocodiles live?

Would you rather be able to make **plants** grow quickly or make it **rain** whenever you want?

It's time to sleep. Would you prefer to lie down in a leaf tent with a **Honduran white bat**...

...or in a grass house with a **harvest mouse**?

Would you rather live to be hundreds of years old like a **cypress tree**...

...or grow to be 9 metres tall like the tallest **sunflower**?

Would you rather munch on **bugs** like a Venus flytrap...

...or be a pitcher plant that eats **frogs**?

Would you rather drink coffee made with **civet poo** or eat durian fruit that smells of **old socks**?

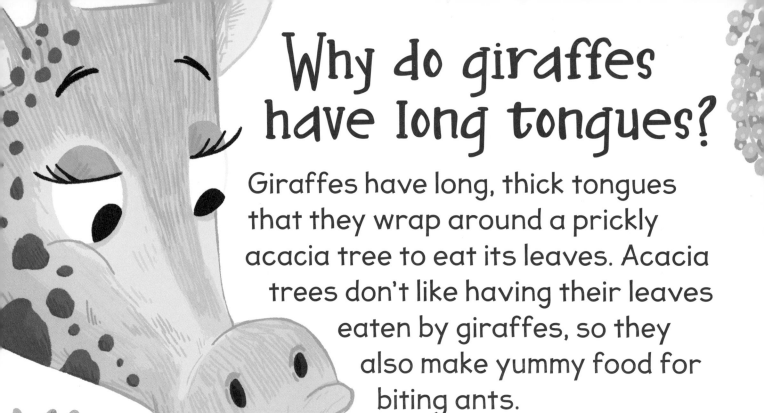

Why do giraffes have long tongues?

Giraffes have long, thick tongues that they wrap around a prickly acacia tree to eat its leaves. Acacia trees don't like having their leaves eaten by giraffes, so they also make yummy food for biting ants.

Ouch!

Durian fruits smell like a mixture of dead fish, smelly socks and poo, but I don't mind. I know the flesh inside is delicious!

If a giraffe tries to eat the acacia leaves we can bite its nose!

Acacia leaves contain sweet nectar that ants love to eat

Yum!

Acacia tree

Why is the durian fruit so smelly?

The big, prickly durian fruit stinks so that animals who like it can easily sniff it out and eat it. They then spread its seeds over a wide area in their poo.

Yum!

Sea slug

Sea grapes seaweed

Why do slugs dress up as plants?

This sea slug looks just like its favourite food — sea grapes seaweed! The slug uses this food to turn itself green and even grows lumps on its back for camouflage as it feeds!

Which plants stink of rotting socks?

Lots of plants make foul smells — and some smell like rotting socks! What's more, some animals love this! Arums often smell like rotting meat to attract flies, which buzz among the arums pollinating them.

My flowers grow 3 metres tall to spread my foul smell far and wide.

Yuk!

Titan arum

How big is the tallest tree?

The tallest tree is a coast redwood called Hyperion in California, USA, and it's taller than a 27-storey building! It is about 116 metres tall, and it grows 4 centimetres taller every year. How much have you grown in the past year?

i have more than 550 million leaves!

(Oast redwood)

Why do people hug trees?

You can hug a tree to work out how big and how old it is. As trees age they get taller but their trunks also get wider. If it takes six children or more to hug an oak tree then it's very old.

Is a mushroom a plant?

No, mushrooms are a type of fungus but, like plants and animals, they are alive. They can grow on dead trees using the wood as their food.

Mushrooms

Warning!
Some mushrooms are very poisonous to eat.

What's that knocking sound?

It's a deathwatch beetle inside rotting wood tapping to attract a mate! In the forest, dead trees and logs make a great place for insects to live and start a family.

I'm tapping on this dead tree so a female can find me! She'll lay her eggs in the rotting wood.

When we hatch from eggs we eat the tasty wood.

Deathwatch beetle

Larvae

131

Who loves plants?

We do! We eat plants. We also use them for lots of other things...

We use **wood** to make paper and cardboard. This book is made from a **tree**!

Oil is made from lots of different plants — such as sunflowers, olives and soybeans — and used for **cooking**.

Rubber is collected from rubber trees. It's turned into lots of things, such as **toys**, tyres and boots.

We use the **wood** from trees to make **furniture**.

Wood is burned to make fires for **cooking** food and for **heating** homes.

Dead plants can be put onto a **compost** heap. When they rot they put nutrients back into the soil, so more plants can grow.

Plants help to **clean our air** by absorbing carbon dioxide, and they help to keep our planet cool, too. This means they can help us to reduce climate change.

Cotton plants grow fluffy cases around their seeds. These are turned into cotton fabric, which is made into **clothes**.

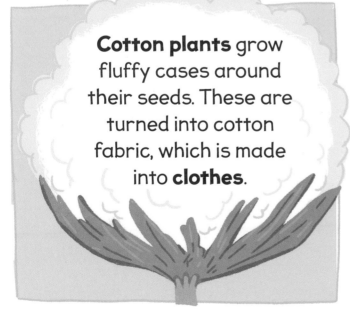

Scientists use plants to make new **medicines** to help treat diseases.

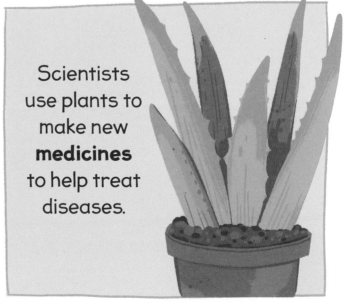

A compendium of questions

Do plants scream?

No, but long ago people believed that a mandrake plant screamed when it was pulled from the ground, and that anyone who heard it would drop dead!

Trees in the Amazon rainforest rely on me to spread their seeds.

Why do people count tree rings?

A tree grows a new ring every year, so you can count the number of rings on a tree stump to see how old it is.

How do piranha fish help rainforests grow?

Some piranhas eat fallen fruit from rainforest trees. They poo out the seeds in the river, which then grow into new trees.

Can a plant live in space?

Yes. On the International Space Station scientists have grown lettuces, peas and courgettes.

Yum!

Why do caterpillars eat poisonous leaves?

Monarch caterpillars eat poisonous milkweed plants and store the poisons in their bodies, so birds won't eat them.

How deep do roots grow?

Plants that grow in very dry places need long roots to reach any water they can find deep in the soil. One fig tree had roots that spread 122 metres down!

What is the largest flower?

The rafflesia plant grows the biggest single flower in the world. It can be more than a metre wide and smells like rotting meat.

Ew!

What's the largest seed in the world?

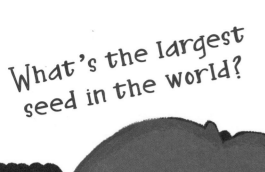

The seeds of a coco-de-mer tree can be 50 centimetres wide and weigh up to 30 kilograms!

My stinky stench attracts carrion flies, which pollinate me.

What is an upside down tree?

Baobabs are sometimes called upside-down trees because their short, thick branches look like roots. They grow smelly flowers to tempt bats to come and pollinate them.

index